Monsters, Myths & Mermaids

Legends of the Sea

This publication may not be reproduced in whole or in part by any
means whatsoever without written permission from the copyright
owners. Permission is never granted for commercial purposes.

Published by
Louis Weber, C.E.O.
Publications International, Ltd.
7373 North Cicero Avenue
Lincolnwood, Illinois 60712

Ground Floor, 59 Gloucester Place
London W1U 8JJ
Customer Service:
1-800-595-8484 or customer_service@pilbooks.com

www.pilbooks.com

8 7 6 5 4 3 2 1

Manufactured in USA.

ISBN-13: 978-1-4508-5621-8
ISBN-10: 1-4508-5621-7

CONTENTS

4   Can You Believe?

6   What's the Scoop on "the Bloop"?

8   Marine Massacre:
     A Devastating Discovery

10   Scene of the Crime: Mass Beachings
     Around the World

12   The One That Got Away:
     Something's Fishy in the Open Sea

14   Splash Speak: How Underwater
     Mammals Communicate

16   Diving Deeper

18   Body of Proof:
     Scientists Continue to Uncover
     Compelling Evidence

20   Tools of the Trade:
     Mermaids' Weapons Include
     Barbs, Spears, and Shells

22   Underwater World

24   Feeding Frenzy: Ocean Friends
     Working Together

26   Dangers of the Deep:
     Trouble Lurks in Murky Waters

28   Survival Story: Supreme Sacrifice

30   Siren Songs: Mermaid Folklore
     Through the Ages

32   Mermaid Mysteries:
     Strange Sightings Have Stumped
     Seafarers for Centuries

34   Monsters & Myths:
     Maritime Monsters

40   Monsters & Myths:
     Map of Monstrous Discoveries

42   Monsters & Myths:
     Do YOU Think These Creatures Exist?

44   NOAA Scientist Q & A:
     Paul Robertson's Stunning Conclusions

46   Monster Quiz:
     Will You Sink or Swim?

48   Glossary

Can You Believe?

Can you believe in things you've never seen... things like dragons, Bigfoot, and the Loch Ness Monster?

What if you found evidence — cold, hard facts — to convince you that fairy-tale creatures do exist?

What you are about to read was enough to convince some scientists that one so-called myth is **actually true.**

Imagine real mermaids swimming in our seas, right alongside dolphins and whales.

Imagine that they managed to stay hidden for thousands of years, and only now is this shimmering possibility slowly rising to the surface.

What if Mermaids Are Real?

What's the Scoop

Three scientists weigh in on an eerie sound.

Dr. Paul Robertson
NOAA Marine Biologist

In 1997, we heard a sound we couldn't identify. It was the most complex, intricate animal call I'd ever heard. And we had no idea what made this sound.

Dr. Rebecca Davis
NOAA Fisheries Department

At the National Oceanic and Atmospheric Administration, or NOAA, we analyze underwater audio recordings. Usually we can easily identify the vocalizations of known marine mammals.

Dr. Rodney Webster
University of South Florida
Animal Communication Specialist

As I analyzed the Bloop, I began to realize that it was nothing like regular animal communication. **They're talking to one another!**

on "the Bloop"?

This strange sound stood out from hundreds of underwater calls and set the stage for a momentous discovery.

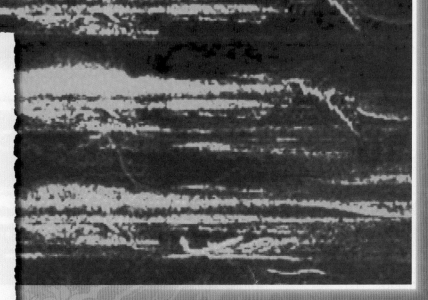

Mystery Sound

In the 50-year history of NOAA's deep-sea acoustic research program, it is the only sound that has *never been identified*.

The recording has been dubbed "the Bloop."

What is the source of the strange wails and otherworldy clicking on this mysterious recording?

Now a team of NOAA scientists believe they have identified the creature making these bizarre cries. **This is their story...**

Marine Massacre

A Devastating Discovery

Scientists started asking tough questions. The result? Truly shocking findings.

Early one morning in 2004, two boys discovered nearly 50 whales stranded on Moclips Beach in Washington state. But as the boys filmed the scene with their camera phone, they saw something else. Authorities quickly removed the creature from the scene, so its identity remained unknown.

Investigators noticed blood coming from the ears of the beached whales. Tissue samples taken from the whales showed **tiny circular lesions**. They believed this to be caused by ultra-low frequency sound waves... a sonar weapon.

What WAS the strange creature captured on the cell phone? Luckily, the phone was one thing authorities did not confiscate.

Scene of the

Great
Britain

Moclips
Beach

North
America

Canada

Cape Cod

North Carolina

South Carolina

Florida

Canary
Islands

Afric

South
America

In the months
that followed,
more mass beachings
were being reported
all over the globe.

Scientists uncovered
a disturbing pattern:
Whale beachings were
occuring near sonar
testing locations. As
they analyzed one of
the audio recordings
of the sonar blasts,
another sound caught
their attention. Right
before the firing
of the sonar weapon,
scientists heard a cry
that was identical to
THE BLOOP!

Crime

Mass Beachings Around the World

Did you know?

Whales, dolphins, and crews on submarines all use forms of sonar. They rely on sound waves to navigate, communicate, and locate objects.

Europe

Asia

Japan

China

"The Bloop" sound surfaced again in South Africa. Was it a warning cry from one creature to another?

Australia

Cape Town

Opoutere Beach

Tasmania

New Zealand

The One That Got Away

Something's Fishy in the Open Sea

Tales of finding fish with spears in them have been circulating since the turn of the century.

Hans Bauer had long heard stories of strange things caught in the Baltic Sea. Sometimes he would even find fish with spears in them.

Where did this spear come from?

As NOAA delved deeper into the mysterious beachings occurring all around the world, they heard about other things, too: stories of unidentified bodies washing up with the whales, rumors of officials always securing the scenes before scientists could get there, reports of fish — caught in the open ocean — with spears in them.

Could a German fisherman named Hans Bauer help the scientists tie all of these strange, separate pieces together?

Did you know?

Fishhooks and fish bones dating back 42,000 years were recently found in a cave in East Timor. This proves that humans have been capable of skilled, deep-sea fishing longer than previously thought.

From Video Footage

Bauer captured an amazing shot on video. Was he infringing on this creature's fishing territory?

13

SPLASH

Talk about deep conversations! Scientists have identified more than 600 signifiers — unique sounds that have meaning — while listening to whales, including humpback whales actually singing in rhyme. That's why "the Bloop" set the scientific community on its ear — it was a sound they had never heard!

Could the Bloop be the sound of mermaids communicating with each other and talking to their whale and dolphin friends?

SPEAK!

How Underwater Mammals Communicate

Did you know?

It's easy for underwater mammals to be on the same wavelength. That's because sound travels more than four times faster in water than it does on land!

Marine mammals such as dolphins and some whales use echolocation, a biological form of sonar.

Diving Deeper

"Possibly one of the most important scientific discoveries in human history."
— Dr. Paul Robertson

What a fluke! The remains included a tail that was unlike anything ever seen!

Researchers hit the jackpot with the discovery of a great white shark that had died off the coast of South Africa. Inside the shark's stomach were the remains of a creature that scientists couldn't identify.

Dr. Robertson noticed puncture marks around the shark's gills — and a stingray barb embedded in the shark! He saved the barb, which turned out to be a valuable clue.

Back in the lab, remains of the mystery creature continued to puzzle researchers. Its hip structure was similar to that of an animal that walks upright. But the reconstructed remains also showed many characteristics common to marine mammals. What was this strange creature?

After ruling out all other possibilities, the scientists came to a shocking conclusion: **It was a new species!**

DNA and dental analysis proved this was NOT a known marine mammal!

Body of Proof: Scientists Continue to Uncover Compelling Evidence

"We were staring in the face of another intelligence."
— Dr. Rebecca Davis

"This creature had hands... like us."
— Dr. Paul Robertson

The research team noticed a concave shape in the front of the skull. The creature's forehead had an organ called a melon, a specialized mass of fatty tissue that enables echolocation. This animal had the ability to emit high frequency sounds, sounds used to communicate with others of its own kind in the deep blue of the vast ocean.

A scan of the reconstructed skull revealed that parts of the brain corresponding to sound interpretation were greatly enlarged. **The scientists now had no doubt that this was the animal that had made the Bloop.**

"Does it have emotion? Does it have empathy?" — Dr. Paul Robertson

Tools of the Trade

Mermaids' Weapons Include Barbs, Spears, and Shells

Did you know?

Dolphins and sea otters use tools, too. Clever dolphins carry marine sponges to stir up the water and uncover prey. And sea otters use stones to hammer open abalone shells!

When Dr. Robertson discovered a carved whale bone among the mermaid remains inside the great white shark, he remembered the stingray barb he'd found earlier. The whale bone and the barb, along with some fibrous plant material, had all fit together as a single item. This was a handmade tool!

The creatures had disarmed stingrays and used their spines as weapons!

Seafarers' stories had told of spears found lodged in fish. Now here was the creature with the dexterity and brain power to construct such tools!

"This was an intelligent tool maker with a grasping hand."
— **Dr. Paul Robertson**

Like their dolphin friends, the mermaids are relatively hairless. Blue pigment helps them blend into their watery world.

They can stay submerged for nearly an hour on a single breath, and a skull ridge helps them dart through the deep water.

Underwater World

With a hinged ribcage to protect their lungs and chest cavities, the creatures' bodies are built to withstand the crushing pressure of the deep.

Did you know?

The world record for holding one's breath underwater belongs to a Swiss freediver who held his breath for almost 20 minutes.

Feeding Frenzy

Ocean Friends Working Together

Echolocation gives dolphins and mermaids the ability to locate food even when there isn't much light to see by. When sounds bounce off a target, the hunt is on. During a sardine run, almost every predator in the ocean will converge on a miles-long caravan of migrating fish. But only dolphins and mermaids work together.

They corral the fish and take turns catching their prey. After a successful hunt, everyone shares in the spoils!

Shared tactics and tools ensure that dolphins and mermaids will get their fill of fish.

Did you know?

There are still a few places on earth where wild dolphins hunt with fishermen. Fishermen call dolphins from the sea and the dolphins respond by driving schools of fish toward the shore.

Dangers of the Deep

Trouble Lurks in Murky Waters

The mermaids are right at home roaming their underwater world. But over the years, they are sure to have faced dangers, too.

Though skilled hunters, mermaids could just as easily become the prey, especially in the days when the now-extinct megalodon, a shark as big as a whale, ruled the ocean.

With the youngest and weakest mermaids unable to escape, what hope would they have of survival?

Mermaids swim hundreds of yards down to hunt in the twilight layer of the sea.

Did you know?

Although shark attacks in the United States declined in 2011, there were 12 worldwide fatalities. This represents the highest number of shark-related deaths in two decades!

A lone scout swims ahead of his pod before they make an open water crossing. They are zeroing in on the deep recesses of dark ocean teeming with schools of fish. These are their feeding grounds. Whales gather here. And so does the mighty megalodon shark.

With the most powerful bite of any creature that ever lived, the megalodon is the greatest threat to the survival of mermaids.

Survival Story

Supreme Sacrifice

They don't see it, but it sees them. The great shark will attack the pod from below.

The shark is drawn to the slowest and most vulnerable. These are the ones it will target.

The scout knows that the pod's survival depends on outwitting the shark. They must be warned. He sounds the alarm.

The scout uses his weapon to cut himself. The shark forgets the pod and follows the smell of blood. The courageous scout is killed instantly. His selflessness has saved his pod from the mighty megalodon!

Siren Songs

Mermaid Folklore Through the Ages

Mermaids and mermen have been a source of fascination throughout history. Merfolk were central characters in Greek mythology. The sea god Triton was often depicted with a man's torso and a fish's tail.

Mermaids have been portrayed as beautiful but dangerous "sirens" whose spellbinding songs lured sailors to their deaths.

The Little Mermaid by Hans Christian Andersen is probably the most famous mermaid story of all time. Like many mermaids of legend, she was blessed with a beautiful singing voice.

Tales of mermaids possessing supernatural powers can be found in ancient mythology.

Little Mermaid Statue
Copenhagen, Denmark

Ancient ships were often adorned with wooden images of beautiful mermaids.

2 บาท BAHT POSTAGE
THAILAND
INTERNATIONAL LETTER WRITING WEEK 1976
สุพรรณมัจฉา SUPHAN-MAT-CHA

Mermaids are frequently depicted combing their long, luxurious hair.

DOMINO
SOLI
GLORIA

Some Irish families actually claim mermaids as their ancestors, and have mermaid images on their family crests and coats of arms.

Mermaid Mysteries

Could sailors have reported seeing mermaids when what they had really glimpsed were swiftly swimming manatees?

As he sailed the high seas, Christopher Columbus reported seeing mermaids playing near what is now Haiti. He was disappointed to see that they "were not as beautiful as painted, although to some they have a human appearance in the face."

The famous explorer Henry Hudson recorded seeing a mermaid near Russia. He said she had long black hair and the tail of a porpoise!

John Smith reported seeing a mermaid off the coast of Massachusetts, although some suspect that he made up the story in order to scare others away from the New World!

Strange Sightings Have Stumped Seafarers for Centuries

Mermaids have been depicted in art all around the world.

Archaeologists believe these cave paintings may be among the oldest mythic images made by man. Do they represent fishermen's dreams, or are they mermaids?

Monsters & Myths

Maritime Monsters

Jumbo jellyfish! Stupendous sturgeons! Yes, sometimes truth IS stranger than fiction, especially when you think about these things swimming among us. And with findings like these, could it be that the kraken and the Loch Ness Monster really DO exist?

In 1954 *The Creature from the Black Lagoon* was released to theaters in 3D.

Coelacanth

Thought to be extinct for more than 65 million years, this "fossil fish" was spotted ALIVE in 1938. There have been more sightings since then, but this creature remains endangered. They can grow up to 6½ feet and weigh up to 200 pounds.

The kraken is a giant sea monster of legend said to dwell off the coasts of Iceland and Norway.

Sturgeon

Residents of Folly Beach, South Carolina, were shocked when an alarmingly large sea creature washed ashore. It turned out to be an Atlantic sturgeon. These fish can grow up to 15 feet in length and weigh 800 pounds!

Giant Jellyfish

Imagine coming face to face with a 6½ foot jellyfish weighing in at almost 450 pounds! Giant Nomura's jellyfish have the capacity to damage nets and poison fish. They have even capsized a fishing boat!

Monsters & Myths

Maritime Monsters

Loch Ness Monster

It's probably the most famous lake monster of all time, but does "Nessie" really roam the dark waters of Scotland's Loch Ness? Is it a giant eel or a long necked seal? Perhaps, like the coelacanth, it's a hardy prehistoric creature that managed to survive extinction. The debate continues…

Since 1933, photos of these creatures have been popping up around the world. Most are hoaxes, but some still remain unexplained.

In 1870, Jules Verne's **Twenty Thousand Leagues Under the Sea** was published. In it, a giant squid attacks the submarine Nautilus.

Titanoboa

The slithering Titanoboa snake stretched longer than a school bus, weighed almost 2,500 pounds, and could easily swallow crocodiles or anything else that stood in its path. Its intimidating name was derived from "titanic" and "boa"—as in boa constrictors!

Giant Squid

Florida fishermen recently netted a catch that was not for the squeamish. It was a 200-pound giant squid floating dead in the Atlantic! But while this was quite a find, scientists say some giant squid can weigh up to a ton!

Monsters & Myths

Maritime Monsters

Megalodon

The great white shark pales in comparison to the mighty megalodon, the largest prehistoric shark that ever ruled the seas. This behemoth is best known for its heart-shaped serrated teeth, each measuring more than an astounding half-foot in size!

Megalodon fossils have been found all over the world. Fossilized teeth are almost all that remains of the megalodon.

In 1851, Herman Melville's *Moby Dick* was published. In it, Captain Ahab seeks revenge on a white whale that destroyed his boat and bit off his leg.

Narwhal

The narwhal is a type of whale that lives near the North Pole. Male narwhals have spiral-shaped tusks that can grow to nearly 9 feet long! The tusk is actually an elongated tooth. Hundreds of years ago, tricky traders charged top dollar for these tusks by claiming they were actually unicorn horns with magical powers.

The boat in the movie *JAWS* is named Orca. An orca is a whale and the only natural predator of great whites.

Monsters & Myths

Greenland Waters

Canadian Arctic

Greenland Waters

North America

Okanagan Lake

West Coast Rivers

Great Lakes

Lake Tahoe

Lake Champlain

Newfoundland

Loch N

Pacific Ocean
(28 – 1.5 million years ago)

Chesapeake Bay

Atlantic Coasts

Missouri and Mississippi Rivers

Jensen Beach

Gulf of Mexico

Pacific Ocean
(28 – 1.5 million years ago)

Colombia
(65 million years ago)

South America

With water covering about 70 percent of the earth's surface, there's no telling what sorts of sea life remain unknown to us.

We already know about the long-gone megalodon and the rediscovered coelacanth. Are Nessie and other legendary creatures actually prehistoric animals that still survive?

As the tales continue to pour in, it's easy to go with the flow and let your imagination run wild!

Map of Monstrous Discoveries

Where are they?

Narwhal

Coelacanth Titanoboa Lake Monster Giant Jellyfish Sturgeon Megalodon Giant Squid

Rivers of Russia
(feeding into the Arctic)

Europe

Asia

Lake Baikal Amur River

Caspian Sea

Black Sea

Lake Van

Lake Tianchi

Rivers of Central Asia

Japan

North & South Korea

China

Africa

Pacific Ocean
(28 ~ 1.5 million years ago)

Pacific Ocean
(28 ~ 1.5 million years ago)

Indonesian coast

Australia

South African Coast

New Zealand

Antarctica

Monsters & Myths

Do YOU Think These Creatures Exist?

So why did the NOAA scientists, who base their work on logic and facts, come to believe in mermaids?

Simple. They found enough data, DNA, and other evidence to convince themselves that mermaids really do exist.

The discovery of the body inside the great white shark was the final piece of the puzzle. They reconstructed its skull, studied its teeth, and analyzed its tail fluke. They came to the shocking conclusion that this was a previously unknown species and the source of the Bloop!

You've read the theories. You've seen what some scientists think. Now it's time to pose the question once again: **Do YOU believe in the existence of mermaids?**

Is it too hard to believe that a creature has stayed hidden from us until now? Even today, the surface of the moon has been explored more than the deepest parts of the ocean. The moon is about 238,857 miles away. The deepest point of the Pacific Ocean, the Mariana Trench, requires a 7 mile journey straight down. But it's a dark, desolate drop to the bottom, with overwhelming water pressure.

Despite such daunting obstacles, ocean exploration is on the rise as researchers, scientists, and even movie directors look to unlock questions about the existence of life miles below sea level. What mysterious creatures might thrive in that seemingly hostile environment?

NOAA Scientist Q & A

Paul Robertson's Stunning Conclusions

Dr. Robertson is a scientist who has been trained to deal in cold, hard facts — not flights of fancy or fairy tales. But a dramatic series of events made him rethink his position on the existence of mermaids. Here's what led Dr. Robertson to come to his startling conclusions.

Q: What was so puzzling about the remains of the body found inside the great white shark?

A: After all this analysis, we'd come up snake-eyes against an entire known inventory of marine mammals. This thing is not a seal. It's not a manatee. And although it talks to dolphins, it's not a dolphin.

Q: What was your "aha!" moment?

A: The discovery that this creature had hands. That changed everything. It would change the way we interpreted this creature. It would change the way we interpret the world.

Q: What would you say to someone who says you just don't have enough evidence?

A: Nature doesn't lie, so look to nature. There are a few places left on earth where wild dolphins hunt with fishermen. And nobody knows how this partnership evolved. Well, we didn't teach dolphins to do this. They taught us. And I think they learned it from someone else. We're not the only culture with a memory of mermaids.

Q: Why did you decide to stop searching for mermaids?

A: I don't want to look for them anymore because they don't want to be found. They have survived because they can hide, so I hope they stay hidden.

Monster Quiz
Will You Sink or Swim?

We've seen how scientists grapple with facts versus fiction. Now it's your turn to unearth the truth. Here are 20 questions that touch on topics found throughout the book. So take a deep breath, settle in, and test your skills!

1 "The Bloop" first surfaced in:

a. 1957
b. 1967
c. 1997

2 "The Bloop" is a:

a. Hamburger
b. Large fish
c. Strange sound made by an unknown creature

3 Moclips Beach is located in:

a. California
b. Washington state
c. Rhode Island

4 Tissue samples taken from beached whales revealed:

a. Tiny circular lesions
b. X and Y chromosomes
c. Acoustic capabilities

5 A narwhal is a:

a. Whale that has a long tusk
b. Type of tropical storm
c. Musical instrument played by singing mermaids

6 What is a megalodon?

a. School of dolphins
b. Mammoth whale
c. Prehistoric shark

7 NOAA scientists believed the mass whale beachings were caused by:

a. Seismic shifts
b. Sonar testing
c. Global warming
d. All of the above

8 A specialized mass of fatty tissue that enables dolphins and whales to echolocate is a:

a. Grape
b. Melon
c. Rutabaga

9 Echolocation is a:

a. Form of bisonar that helps give marine mammals a mental map of their environment
b. NOAA device that tracks underwater sounds and signifiers
c. Sailor's high-pitched distress signal
d. None of the above

10 NOAA scientists hit the jackpot when they found this in South Africa:

a. Krugerrand
b. Great white shark
c. Megalodon tooth

11 NOAA stands for:

a. National Organization of Astronauts and Astronomers
b. National Oceanic and Atmospheric Administration
c. Natural Ocean and Aviation Association

12 Titanoboa is a:

a. Gigantic snake
b. Very strong metal
c. Type of submarine
d. None of the above

13 Approximately what percentage of the earth is comprised of water:

a. 70 percent
b. 60 percent
c. 50 percent

14 About how many signifiers for whales have scientists recorded:

a. 1,000
b. 600
c. 286

15 The kraken is a:

a. Legendary sea monster
b. Small fish often used as bait
c. Male sea lion

16 A mermaid's lungs are said to be protected by:

a. Fashioned bones
b. Hinged ribcage
c. Tail fluke

17 How much faster does sound travel through water than air:

a. 2 times
b. 8 times
c. 4 times

18 Which famous explorer was disappointed in the mermaid's appearance:

a. Christopher Columbus
b. Henry Hudson
c. Ferdinand Magellan

19 Dolphins and mermaids work together to:

a. Chase sharks
b. Build homes
c. Catch fish

20 It's been said that mermaids lure sailors to their death by:

a. Diving
b. Singing
c. Dancing

Turn the page for the answer key.

Score Key

0-5 Correct
You're megalodon bait

6-10 Correct
Possible beaching ahead

11-17 Correct
Swimming in sonar-free waters

18-20 Correct
You're NOAA material

NO peeking!

Glossary

Coelacanth "Fossil fish" that was discovered off the African coast in 1938.

DNA Abbreviation for deoxyribonucleic acid, which contains genetic information about organisms.

Fluke A lobe on a marine mammal's tail that helps propel it through water. Flukes are made of muscle and dense fibrous tissue.

Echolocation Biological sonar that enables marine mammals to send out high-frequency sounds that bounce off objects and give the animal a mental map of the environment.

Megalodon A prehistoric shark generally considered the most terrifying predator in history.

Melon A specialized mass of fatty tissue that allows dolphins and whales to echolocate.

National Oceanic and Atmospheric Administration (NOAA) A scientific agency that is part of the U.S. Department of Commerce. Its responsibilities include managing fisheries and issuing storm warnings.

Pod A group of dolphins or whales swimming together in a social group.

"The Bloop" The first unidentifiable sound in the history of NOAA's deep-sea acoustic research program.

Sonar Underwater sound waves used to detect and locate submerged objects or measure the distance to the floor of a body of water.

Quiz Answer Key

1. c	6. c	11. b	16. b
2. c	7. b	12. a	17. c
3. b	8. b	13. a	18. a
4. a	9. a	14. b	19. c
5. a	10. b	15. a	20. b